LIVERPOOL
IN A CITY LIVING 2

Top Left: Sitting on the steps on the corner of Holly Street and Christian Street in 1966

Top Right: In St. John's Gardens. The cranes in the background are constructing St. John's Shopping Precinct

Bottom Left: At the Steble Fountain. Buses could then go up William Brown Street and Islington.

Bottom Right: Standing by the swings on Christian Street. McDougall's funeral parlour is in the background.

In this volume the author has enhanced his text by including various poems and lyrics descriptive of Liverpool life in the period.

Should he have indvertently infringed any copyright he apologises and asks that the copyright holder will contact him through the publisher's office in order that due acknowledgement may be made in future editions.

First Published 2005 by Countyvise Limited,
14 Appin Road, Birkenhead, Wirral CH41 9HH

Copyright © 2005 Gerard Fagan

The right of Gerard Fagan to be identified as the author of this work has been asserted by him in accordance with the Copyright, Design and Patents Act 1988.

British Library Cataloguing in Publication Data.
A catalogue record for this book is available from the British Library.

Please note: From 1st January 2007 ISBNs will contain 13 numbers. These numbers will be the same as the present number printed below the barcode (ie. starting 978).
Countyvise is showing both existing (10 digit) and future (13 digit) ISBNs on the Title page verso. Please continue to use the 10 figure number until 31st December 2006.

ISBN: 1 901231 56 9   ISBN: 978 1 901231 56 4

DEDICATION

This book is dedicated to my mam and dad, Nora and Joe, without whom none of this would have been possible of course.

Special thanks to my wife Ann Marie and children Melanie, Melissa and Katy for their patience and understanding whilst I was busy researching.

I would also like to express my sincere thanks to the following:

Kay Parrott of the Central Library Records Office and the search room team for their efforts with the supplying of photographs and the information for use in this book. For information on their archive, contact www.mersey-gateway.org/pastliverpool

Stephen Hemsworth for his time and efforts in formatting my data.

Paul Sudbury, a fellow ex Gerard Crescenter, for his time and efforts in the supply of photographs, information and his computer wizardry.

The Liverpool Daily Post and Echo, for their support. www.icliverpool.com

Ron Formby of the Scottie Press, for his information, interest and publicising of my project. Contact ronformby@scottiepress.org with any local information.

My brother Joe, still not a priest, but an inspiration for ideas.

Derrick Fielding at Mersey Memories, see the last few pages of the book. For your own Mersey Memory personal street guide contact derrickfielding65@hotmail.com

Joan and Paul at the Lord Warden, London Road and Lil and Bev at Burgess PDQ, Christian Street for their kind supply of photographs.

Last but not least John at Countyvise and his team, for their assistance and time taken in the preparation and publication of this book.

All songs lyrics and poems reproduced are Copyright of the Composers or their publishing companies.

FAGO GOES TO THE BIG SCHOOL

In 1973 and fast approaching 11 years of age, the 11+ was coming up. An exam which would determine which 'big' school you would be attending in September. Rumour had it that if you passed, you'd be stranded, out on your own, away from your mates, attending some la di da school like the Collegiate up in Shaw Street. Well, this imposing castle like building conjured up images of Tom Brown's schooldays, the birch and more worryingly, hard work!

My birthday was the end of August making me the youngest in the class, another few days and I'd have missed being included in the new intake of pupils, as we always seemed to go back around the 5th of September.

Goodbye St. Joey's. Bishop Goss Junior School. We were sometimes allowed on the roof and could see Bidston Windmill on Wirral as well as Moel Famau in the distance. The new assembly and dinner hall (to the right) were erected whilst we were there in the late 1960s.

Needless to say, 99% of the Saint Joey's (Bishop Goss) class of 73 went onto Saint Gregory's Secondary School, the upper School having been opened just a few years earlier on nearby Prince Edwin Street.

The intake for St. Greg's would generally consist of pupils from the Junior Schools of Bishop Goss, St. Anthony's, The Friary and a handful from Holy Cross. On the very first day, one of our lads from St. Joey's was sent out from the assembly hall for the cane. One nil to St. Joey's and welcome to the big school - No messing about here.

The route to our 'new' school for us Gerard Gardens and Gerard Crescenters took us along Christian Street, past the swings or should I say, the remnants of the old playground which was next to McDougall's funeral parlour, across Saint Anne Street and through the forecourt of the new John Wallwork Volvo car showrooms which is now Arnold Clarke. It would be normal to gaze into the showroom and marvel at those giant Volvo saloon and Estate cars, the 240, new to the UK market with their larger than life bumpers.

Realising the headmaster, Mr. Crowley would be prowling the reception area, cane in one hand, a bunch of keys in the other, ready to lock you out if a second late, we would quickly gather our thoughts together, as someone asking the time remarked, 'we'd better get a move on'. There was still the walk up Prince Edwin Street to negotiate, it would seem like hours, past the little white prefabs which were situated just in front of the old landing dwellings on the right hand side of the street.

The reception housed huge shields on the wall facing the entrance. These portrayed images of the four forms for each year. St.Aiden, St. Augustine, St. Bede and St. Columba. From here, at 9am we would be

Hello St. Greg's. St Gregory's Roman Catholic Secondary Modern, seen here from its main entrance in Prince Edwin Street, Liverpool 5. This school is now called Campion and was recently under the threat of closure.

ushered into the assembly hall to the screams of 'Don't run, don't run' from Matty, the caretaker, where Mr. Crowley would cast an evil eye over their motley crew.

1974 saw us touring Churches such as St. Anthony's, the Friary and St. Teresa's, Norris Green with our rendition of Joseph and his Technicolour Dreamcoat, I mean 1974…Jason Donovan eat your heart out. We, in the 1st year had to sing in the choir whilst those in the 5th year got to act the parts on stage. I have memories of the music teacher, Mr. Connolly, trying to get melodic singing out of us. His classroom had chairs with an attachment to the armrest where you could write your notes, but my lasting memory of him is that he had a metal tipped cane - masochist!

Now if you think he had problems getting us to sing in English, imagine the uphill task faced by Miss Ryan in trying to get us to sing in French in her French classes.

St Greg's side view from China Street park on Netherfield Road

Swimming lessons were taken at Margaret Street Baths. We'd usually have a bus to take us but I remember on more than one occasion having to walk. They were the old style lockers, along the side of the pool. One time, we were told to come out of the locker and to stand alongside the pool where we were. Mr Cooper, another masochist, informed us that the 5-a-side goals had been damaged back at the lower school gym and this class was suspected. We were to bend over, alongside the pool, take a whacking thump of the pump, which was Mr Cooper's smelly old baseball shoe and then fall into the water. Now, if the prospect of this didn't bring water to your eyes, literally, imagine how I felt. As one of the last off the bus, my locker was up the six foot end of the pool. What's the problem you may ask ? 'I can't swim sir' I yelled. This fell on deaf ears as I fell in the water taking more on board than the Titanic. Can you imagine that these days, Mr. Cooper would be facing the European Court of Human Rights.

Mr Cooper was one you couldn't mess with. I think he and Mr Huxam, the other P.E. teacher would have made a good T.V. cop duo playing the good guy and the bad guy. Cooper, or Mick to his friends, so we'll call him Cooper, was definitely more rugby orientated, I mean he wore a rugby shirt every day, and yes, usually the same one, pwoaar - Mr Cooper would have gone down well in somewhere like Merchant Taylors, I wish he had gone down there. A trend-setter all the same, he had his sparse top lip growth long before Terry Sullivan on Brookside. He was famed for having a crush on the girl's P.E. teacher, Miss Coates, much to Mr Huxam's amusement who often instigated the whispers and leg pulling himself.

Stevie Huxam. If there's such a thing as a man's man then he was a real lad's teacher. You knew when you could have a joke with him depending on his attire. If he had his tracksuit on, it was O.K. On the rare occasion he was suited up, he was in a serious mood. Also our Geography teacher, he was known to leap up in his top floor classroom and kick the world globe which was hanging from the ceiling, such was his agility. In his guise as Geography teacher we would go on occasional field trips in the School's Ford Transit Minibus, a very 70s light blue with maroon stripe, I wonder if that's where Starsky and Hutch got their idea ? - No, I think not.

The trips I remember with fondness were to Star Crossing and Butlins in Pwllheli, both in Wales and to the shore and common at Thurstaston on Wirral, which itself seemed miles away at the time. Mr Huxam possessed a mean orange VW Beetle with zany black stripes on the bonnet and roof.

This double act of Cooper and Huxam would sometimes send us out on a run. This would take us down 'Prinny Eddy' onto 'Greaty' and back up Roscommon Street past the Farmers Arms pub which was a few doors away from the one time abode of Herbert Morton Stanley of 'Dr. Livingstone I presume' fame. Past the Cotton Picker pub on the other corner and back into the school gates with still time for a game of footy. It certainly beat the ropes, wallbars and horse vaulting which I hated.

In 1975, my second year at Greg's, asbestos was discovered in part of the building and we had to move lock, stock and barrel into nearby Roscommon Street School. This included literally carrying your desk the short distance to Rossy. The advantage here for the P.E. lesson was that Rossy came with its own big footy pitch at the rear of the school, albeit a concrete one but at least it had goals.

Mr Liddiard was one of our woodwork teachers. He had a white Saab and collected Samouri swords. More annoyingly for us though was that he soaked his cane in an aluminium tube of linseed oil to give it an extra toughness when trying to break our fingers. The tube was held vertically in the vice of one of the woodwork benches. Are you getting the impression yet that this school was more like a torture chamber if you stepped out of line. I'll tell you what though, few did.

The other woodwork teacher and ex army man was old Mr. Quinn with the smooth planed chin. His favourite call to his class was to 'fall in'. This meant we all had to assemble around his woodwork bench at the head of the class whilst he proceeded to show us how to do a dove-tail or mortice and tenon joint, paying particular attention to the 'smooth edge'. Little did these teachers know that MFI, B&Q and Texas Homebase would be selling flatpack furniture (with extra screws) within the next few years so there was no need to be making these teapot stands and jewellery boxes.

Whilst the boys were learning woodwork, or maybe not, the girls were under the supervision of Miss Scott who was undertaking domestic science classes which to you and I is cookery. Since I never got the chance to hone my skills over the cooker, I can lay the blame fairly and squarely on Miss Scott that I now struggle to cook a soft boiled egg. Her blue VW beetle wasn't as eye catching as Mr Huxam's either.

Miss Blundell and the lanky one, Miss Clarke, were our art teachers who helped me to a grade 1 C.S.E. However, I could also say that the great invention of tracing paper played its part in the case of my project work. If only she knew, she may now.

Des King was the Science teacher and his lessons were looked forward to, if only for the fact it was a chance to sneak into the lab technicians office afterwards whilst the rest of the class had to go to break. Harry, the lab tech was a walking mop of black hair, he also had a muzzy and goatie. Being the only human in the school nearest to our age group, he was classed as cool. The fact he let us help him make stink bombs and exploding bangers probably helped as well. Mr King's lessons would by and large consist of a projector showing a pre-written lesson onto his white board. Bunsen burners, test tubes and crucibles would have been set out by Harry, pre-lesson and we would have to write a description of the experiment together with a conclusion. The only conclusion we ever reached unanimously was that Des used to turn off the engine to his Austin A40 and roll down Prinny Eddy at about 8.50 a.m. - Honest he did. Mr. Rice, the other, larger, science teacher left before we did thus saving our legs from any further welts, as his punishment was to whip the backs of your legs with the rubber hose from the bunsen burners, thank you my old mate Brian for remembering that one.

If ever there was occasion for one of the female teachers to send you for the 'stick' (the cane), you hoped it would be to Mr. Crowley and not Mr. Grocott. The Brothers Crowley were the headmaster and his clone with matching Rover cars in white and brown. The stockier of the two, and I'm being kind here, had a great singing voice though. 'Christus vincit, Christus regnat, Christus imperat used to echo through the assembly hall. Mr. Grocott who everyone knew early on as Lenny (but had the total respect of the masses that nobody ever called him it to his face) was possibly the nicest bloke and certainly the favourite of the many ex pupils I've spoken to. He had the reputation of the hardest cane giver though it is equally true that you really had to have upset someone in order to get a taste of it from him.

Mr Forshaw was my Religious Education teacher. I got a grade 1 in this too which together with my Art grade 1 came in handy for drawing holy pictures. Not really, just a bit of sarcasm there you see. He usually had the lesson pretty much already marked out for you on the blackboard as you took your seat. His window looked out onto Netherfield Road so it was quite handy for seeing the Orange Lodge marching along from time to time. Also from his window you could see the China Street club and play area which were frequented some dinner times by the locals and moi.

Mr Murphy was the maths teacher. If I could speak to him just once more, I wouldn't mind asking what all those logarithms, anti-logarithms and algebra lessons were for and whereabouts in everyday life they might one day come in handy ? It was whispered that he kept a half flagon of scotch in his drawer but no one had the bottle, if you pardon the pun, to prove it or otherwise. I personally blame the purple nose on poor circulation.

Mr McNulty was a decent teacher if memory serves me correctly, that's debatable of course, depending on whom you ask. What's not debatable is that he was famed for having a nailed on wig and glasses like the bottom of milk bottles.

Mr Hart was known to throw the odd blackboard duster at you if you weren't paying attention. He was also known to throw the even one too. You generally didn't mess in his lessons as wood tends to hurt if thrown at your head at 60 m.p.h.

In the third year of Greg's and with the thought that we weren't even quite halfway through our sentence yet, a few of us were contemplating contacting the Samaritans. Then, a ray of light. The

Education authorities sent a couple of relief/temp teachers who you could throw blackboard dusters at instead. Mr Hulme made an impression with his high pitched falsetto voice during hymn singing to the point where we had to be grateful for reinforced glass in the windows of the assembly hall. Mr Duggan wore velvet jackets that were ideal for throwing lumps of powder paint at which we'd smuggle out of Miss Blundells art class. These paint bombs would explode between his shoulder blades, sometimes without him even knowing. We believed that what he didn't know wouldn't hurt him but I bet his washing machine churned out some lovely psychedelic looking tee-shirts and I'm sure I saw him selling them from a stall at the last Beatles convention.

Miss Healy and Miss Copeland I'm sure were lovely ladies but being younger and newer to the school they tended to let you get away with murder. Definitely the female versions of Hulmy and Duggan. Miss Allen had also arrived at the school by now and quickly became deputy head. She stood for no nonsense and once locked us in our class after last lesson until someone owned up to some misdemeanour.

Bishop Goss pupils commemorating the retirement of Miss Brockbank after nearly 50 years of teaching at the school. This was taken in 1968.

Most of us received a similar reference upon departing in 1978. I think Mr. Crowley just had a stamp made with '……….. has attended this school for the last blah blah blah' and then inserted your name in the appropriate gap. It was in the days before you could save your document in 'Word' of course. I was going to mention it was done on a typewriter, only younger readers will be asking their parents 'what's a typewriter ?'

Other teachers that were at the school at some time or another, but not for the whole of our stay were Miss Garner, Miss Leahy, Miss Parry and Mr. Addison. Due to this, they manage to escape the venom of my typing finger - lucky them. Father Cunningham was the School Chaplain for much of our stay at Greg's.

It wasn't all that bad though you know, all part of the learning curve, all part of life's journey. Let me take you on another journey now. For what it was like for our forefathers growing up in our area and then the improvements that were made which must have seemed like luxury for them, but for us, well we knew no different.

'Our Day Out' - This motley crew from the bottom end of the square were assembled for an organised day trip to Southport in 1969. The photo was taken from the landing in Gerard Crescent.

IN THE TOWN

The Wellington Column and the Steble Fountain, dating back from 1863 and 1875 respectively. Viewed from the roof of Saint George's Hall, Commutation Row here consists of thirteen properties, the last three being eventually demolished on the corner of London Road and replaced with the Burton's building.

Living in the Gerard Gardens area, less than ten minutes walk from the city centre, meant you had practically everything on your doorstep. Whether it be St. John's Gardens for games of hide n' seek, football or riding your bike or off to the Art Gallery or Museum just to pass the time.

Shopping wasn't such a chore, especially when it was a trip to Hobbies or City Models or one of the big stores like Lewis' or Blacklers.

From our landing in the square, you could follow the construction progress of St. John's Beacon and the like. Here are just a few views of the city centre area as we knew it and which was so close to the heart of the inner city kids.

IN MY LIVERPOOL HOME
(P. McGOVERN)

I was born in Liverpool down by the docks,
My religion was Catholic, occupation - hard knocks,
At stealing from lorries, I was adept,
And under old overcoats each night I slept.

In my Liverpool home, in my Liverpool home,
We speak with an accent exceedingly rare,
Meet under a statue exceedingly bare,
And if you want a Cathedral, we've got one to spare,
In my Liverpool home.

Back in the forties, the world it went mad,
And Hitler, he threw at us all that he had,
When the smoke and the dust had all cleared from the air,
'thank god' said my old man, 'the Pier Head's still there,'

In my Liverpool home, in my Liverpool home,
We speak with an accent exceedingly rare,
Meet under a statue exceedingly bare,
And if you want a Cathedral, we've got one to spare,
In my Liverpool home.

William Brown Street. looking east into Islington. The spire is that of Saint Francis Xavier's on Salisbury Street.

Commutation Row rooftops, showing the rear of warehouse property on Camden Street

London Road in 1966. No buses, then nine come at once. Plenty of road markings too for the Pier Head and Tunnel.

London Road in 1949 at the junction with Commutation Row and Lime Street. Montague Burton's clothing store, which was issuing the 'Full Monty' demob suits after the end of WWII, four years earlier, stands proud. On the opposite corner, the original Legs of Man Public House. There is a traffic Policeman on directional duties.

A view of Saint George's Hall in 1895 showing Saint John's Church. In 1767 a new burial ground on a heath near to the infirmary (the current site of the Saint George's Hall) was consecrated as Saint John's churchyard. The town at this point was divided into five wards. Saint Nicholas's, Saint George's, Saint Peter's, Saint Thomas's and Saint. John's. On 24th June 1775 the foundation stone for Saint John's Church was laid, the design being of Gothic style executed by architect Thomas Litoller. It was completed and consecrated in 1784. The Churchyard itself was to house over 27,000 graves before it closed for interment in 1854. Just three years after the above photograph was taken, the last service was held at the church and the site was acquired by the Liverpool Corporation for laying out of St. John's Gardens in 1904.

MAGGIE MAY
(TRADITIONAL)

O Maggie, Maggie May, they have taken her away
And she'll never walk down Lime Street anymore.
O she robbed those lime juice sailors and the captains of the whalers,
That dirty no good robbing Maggie May.

O the first time I saw Maggie, she took my breath away,
She was cruising up and down old Canning Place,
She'd a figure so divine, like a frigate on the line,
So me being a sailor, I gave chase.

In the morning I awoke, I was flat and stony broke,
No jacket, waistcoat, trousers could I find,
And when I asked her 'where', she said, 'my very good sir',
'they're down in Kelly's pawnshop number nine.

O Maggie, Maggie May, they have taken her away,
And she'll never walk down Lime street anymore,
For the judge he guilty found her, for robbing the homeward-bounder,
That dirty no good robbing Maggie May.

Saint George's Place. As busy as ever but not a carbon monoxide fume in the air. I should imagine the Corporation refuse department were kept well busy though with the amount of horse manure that must have been around.

William Brown Street Victoriana. A blind lady stands at the gates of Saint John's churchyard near Saint George's Hall van passage. The ladies look rather more elegantly dressed than the men folk.

Bold Street. As busy as ever. The Lyceum, built in the reign of King George III in 1802 is located bottom left. This Street has been pedestrianised for some time now.

CHRISTMAS TIME IN CHURCH STREET
(G. FAGAN)

The hustle and the bustle of taxis and buses,
The crisp snow in Church Street, the people there rushing.
Woolie's is packed to the brim with kids shopping,
With mams and dads close by, they're ready for dropping.

Toys on display, kerplunk, crossfire and lotto,
As Santa greets innocents in Blackler's grotto,
The Tatler is showing Burl Ives nearby,
'There was an old woman who swallowed a fly'.

Dusk falls as shoppers spill out on the street,
Marks and Sparks, Bunneys, Bon Marche, people meet.
Heading for bus stops, Longview and Lyme Cross,
Corpies, Crosvilles and Ribbles, to places now lost.

Church Street in January 1965. With Christmas just gone, the January sales are in full swing. The No. 86 Garston Circular 'corpy' bus is making its way back to the Pier Head terminus.

Those from over the water make tracks to the Lanny,
Where the Woodchurch and Daffodil lay waiting for many,
Excited the children will chitter and chatter,
But weary limbs dictate there's no pitter patter.

In front of the fire on this cold winters night,
Now safely home much to mother's delight,
And so off to sleep, tummy full, pleasant dreams,
About the day past, is this what Christmas means?

Crosshall Street/Dale Street junction. The American Enterprise Hardware Co. selling amongst other things, Yale locks and latches. Up until recently it was the longstanding home of another tool suppliers and ironmongers, Thomas & Nelson. Next door, you could 'seek or sell' any out of print books.

Saint John's Beacon, under construction in 1970. Viewed from the roof of Central Station, looking North along Cases Street. The structure stands 450 feet above sea level, 335 feet above Liverpool City Centre. it was opened on April fools day 1971, some say, quite ironically. As part of Saint John's Shopping Precinct, it housed a revolving restaurant and observatory deck giving unrivalled 360 degree panoramic views of city and beyond. After a massive fire at the precinct in 1977, the tower was closed and lay dormant as stringent safety regulations were implemented. Plan after plan failed to see a grand re-opening but it is now home to Liverpool's Radio City who took residence there, having started life in October 1974 as 194 Radio City in nearby Stanley Street.

THE HUNTER STREET AREA

In the mid 1800s, Liverpool was competing, knowingly or otherwise, with other Lancashire towns and cities such as Blackburn, Bolton and Manchester for the grandest architecture for its civic buildings. The characteristics of such buildings during this period was of a Neo Grecian style.

Whilst Sir William Brown and Sir Andrew Barclay Walker were providing massive funding for the Liverpool Museum and Art Gallery respectively in William Brown Street, just behind what was to become the grandest façade in the whole of the city lay a poverty stricken area with insanitary property and slum ridden courts housing destitute families and barefoot street urchins.

Nearly a decade earlier, St George's Hall had gone fantastically over budget to the tune of 80K, a massive amount in those days, but still there were no plans in place to improve the squalid living conditions, which were so prevalent nearby.

Dr. W. Duncan, having been appointed as the Liverpool Medical Officer governing health (the first in the UK), very soon ascertained that the average age of death in Liverpool at this time was just seventeen years of age with over half of all deaths being in infancy. This was the highest in the UK and in particular it was pinpointed to the Scotland Road area of the city centre.

From Hunter Street at the rear of William Brown Street to Richmond Row in the north and from Byrom Street up to Christian Street, not a large area, more than 50 streets and courts existed. These were populated to the brim with locals and swelled by the massed ranks of Irish and Italian immigrants who settled here collectively between 1847 and 1912.

In 1922 a motion was tabled by the Liverpool Corporation to look into the feasibility of a Mersey road crossing. After much discussion about whether a bridge or underground tunnel would be most appropriate, a decision was made to clear the nearby west side of the old Haymarket and set about what was to become an amazing feat in civil engineering. From 1925 to 1934 and at a cost of £8 million, the biggest single municipal enterprise ever undertaken in the country was underway.

In 1933, Dixie Dean's victorious Everton had paraded the F.A. cup around William Brown Street on a horse drawn carriage, this after defeating Manchester City 3-0 at Wembley in a game that was to see shirt numbers worn for the first time. Everton were numbered 1 to 11, Manchester City 12 to 22.

It is hard to imagine that whilst life seemingly went on, just a stone's throw away, deprivation of an unequalled parallel existed. It is little wonder that the Liverpool Corporation eventually embarked on a slum clearance programme throughout the city that would take many years to have the desired effect. The Corporation's Engineers Department would carefully photograph and catalogue the most deprived areas where many were enduring unhealthy and cramped conditions.

Shops, factories and public houses existed in this vicinity side by side with the squalor. Running along Byrom Street northwards from the Technical College, prior to their demolition were the following premises.

On the north corner of Clayton Street was The Clayton Arms public house at No.18, then the whole block up to Cuerden Street which was No.20 to 26 was taken up by W & T Avery Ltd who were weighing machine manufacturers. On the north side of Cuerdon Street at No. 28 was another weighing machine manufacturers called Berry & Warmington. Next door to this property at No. 30 was the Unique Café and overhead was the Temperance Hotel. On the corner of Hunter Street was the Byrom Arms Public House at Nos 32-34, which was formerly known as the Iron Duke.

On the opposite corner of Hunter Street were Leicester Buildings. This was occupied by the Scotland Road branch of the Spice Mill Co. Heading up Hunter Street was the weights and measures office (which obviously played a large part in this area.) Next to that were W. Jones & Co. Ltd, which was a printing works.

Back onto Byrom Street and beyond Cartwright Place stood Saint Stephen's Church. The original building dated from 1722 stood nearby and it was documented that it was a chapel used by 'that respectable sect of Christians - the Baptists.' and later 'a meeting place for dissenters'. It is further reported that in 1789 they moved to 'a more commodious structure' in Gerard Street, (Byrom Hall). In 1792 they sold the old chapel to the Church of England and it was subsequently opened on 18th March that year as St. Stephen's Church.

In 1868 it was recorded to have been 'for upward of thirty years, one of the best attended churches in Liverpool' but was now surrounded by the poorer classes of our population, the greater portion of the respectable tradesmen and shop-keepers being non-resident in the district. In 1870 Byrom Street was widened, St Stephen's was closed after the last service on 31st July that year. A new building was erected, the site being consecrated on 5th August 1870 by the Bishop of Chester.

Eventually in 1920 the church took over the parish of Christ Church on Hunter Street (which dated from 1797 then subsequently closed) but St. Stephens itself was only to last another seventeen years when its benefices and parishes were united with St. Anne's, Richmond on St. Anne Street. Liverpool Corporation subsequently purchased the church and the site for £9000 in 1938 where it succumbed to yet another street widening scheme.

Across Byrom Terrace was Hathaway's toy shop at No. 52, Stephen Crute's hairdressing saloon at No. 54 and Wilson's laundry Ltd at No. 56. John Simon Roberts, fried fish dealers came next at No. 58, Henry Eymond tobacconist at No. 60 and Banner's Pure Drug Co. Ltd Chemists at No. 62. On the corner of Gerard Street was the Grapes Inn public house.

Across Gerard Street was Byrom Hall, home to the Liverpool City Mission, next door was the Army & Navy stores and then not unusually, on the corner, yet another Public House, the Dunbar Castle. Across Circus Street, the property angled off north east up Richmond Row at the junction with Scotland Place. At this point there was a further number of public houses, namely the Birmingham Arms, the Old Cabbage and the Morning Star.

In amongst the housing of this densely populated area were the ever welcoming corner shops such as Lunt's up on Christian Street,

The rear of 48 Circus Street, taken on 25th June 1933. By now, children are wearing footwear and nine locals pose here for the camera, (check out the man in his backyard.) The property itself is in a state of disrepair and part of the raised waste ground to the rear of the yards is eroded away which must have resulted in flooding when it rained. It was common for the residents to white wash the walls to brighten the place up a bit and reflect the sunlight into their windows.

Santangeli's ice cream parlour on Bennett Street and Lovell's on Whale Street. Commercial property on Circus Street consisted of Bigland's Bakery Supplies Ltd and Roger's the noted welders whilst on Feather Street there were Spice Mills and at the Holly Street junction with Downe Street, E.R. Owen & Co. sack merchants operated alongside Bowden's Refrigeration Company.

John Brodie, the City Engineer (and incidentally, inventor of the goal net in 1890) was to be in charge of the slum clearance project. He was responsible for such masterpieces as the Queen's Drive inner ring road, the East Lancashire Road and prefabricated concrete buildings of 'clinker' as in the Eldon Street dwellings of 1905. His idea for tramcars to use a central reservation was also inaugurated on a stretch in Broadgreen in 1914 and now he was controlling the massive Queensway Tunnel enterprise.

The plan was to create communities living in 3, 4 and 5 storey walk up flats, usually built in blocks that would create a centre square or circle. Within, such delights as a children's playground would be created together with shrubs, trees and flower beds and as such they would be called 'Gardens'. Some tenements, as they became known, would house shops and even a chapel of rest as in Caryl Gardens.

By the time many plans and proposed drawings for the Hunter Street/Byrom Street area were submitted in the 1930s, Lancelot Keay (later Sir) who had been

REAR OF 48 CIRCUS ST.
(GERARD ST AREA.)

Brodie's assistant since 1925 was in office as the housing chief and city architect. The tenements were to be in an art deco style, a feature of this period. On 21st June 1935 the Rt Hon Sir Kingsley Wood M.P. the Minister of Health laid the foundation stone for the Gerard Gardens complex.

Although other tenements preceded this, he declared that this was to be a 'Great scheme for housing the people'. The main arched entrance on the Hunter Street/Christian Street junction was to be elevated, a great curved flight of steps stretching out before it. Upon entering the square you would be at a raised level, partly because of the aforementioned elevation and partly because the land to the West fell away in a natural slope. Three flights of stairs, one to the south, another to the north and another in the centre would take you down to ground level within the 'square'.

Hunter Street Courts on the 7th November 1933. More, three storey property accessed across a paved area. The far corner dwelling has its front door housed at an angle. One lone gas lamp in situ would illuminate the area and a gutter runs down one side of the yard from a single water tap.

By 1937 Gerard Gardens was complete. Much of the property to its west had been demolished and the mid section of Gerard Crescent, which mirrored the curve of Gerard Gardens was also in place. However, dilapidated property to its north on Christian Street still existed as did the Quakers Friends Meeting House dating from 1796 and its burial ground on Hunter Street, preventing any further progress in that direction. By 1939 the four blocks of Cartwright, Lionel, Downe and Thurlow House were erected in that order, built on streets of the same name that were cleared in the previous 3 years.

Satisfied with the regeneration of the area, Sir Lancelot Keay commissioned 'the builder' and 'the architect' figures in Portland stone from sculptor, Herbert Tyson Smith. They were to adorn the entrances to Gerard Gardens.

It was not until as late as 1942 that the Friends Meeting House was flattened. Photographs taken in 1945 show the site ready to be built on, allowing for a further arch to be added to the Crescent for easier access to Gerard Gardens as well as space for another twenty nine flats to be added to the block. On Hunter Street itself, a totally different type of accommodation was to be constructed. By 1950, new style three storey flats were springing up all over the city, these now considered to be a further improvement on the tenement style dwellings. Gerard Close with its 12 flats and enclosed landings completed the development.

The rest of the clearance area to the rear of Thurlow, Downe, Lionel and Cartwright House was earmarked for the new Technical College which took up residence on the whole of the east side of Byrom Street from Hunter Street to Richmond Row. This was built between 1957 and 1960 with an extension added in 1969.

In 1952, the first proposals were drawn up for an idea consisting of an inner city ring road with flyovers. The flyovers were not to be where they are situated at present, but rather, one at the bottom of London Road and one off the newly extended Christian Street, crossing over Scotland road and on into Leeds Street. It was to be the late 60s before the flyovers as we know them now were erected.

Byrom Street, seen here from Byrom Terrace to Gerard Street. Taken on the 9th March 1931, the properties are, at No. 52 Hathaway's toy shop advertising wholesale merchandise. Stephen Crute's hairdressing saloon where you can have a haircut and shave for 6d is at No. 54. Wilson's Laundry Ltd is next door at 56 where you could get your shirt and collar starched using 'Robin Starch'. John Simon Robert's the fried fish dealer's is at No. 58 and you can get your newspapers and cigarettes at No. 60, which is Henry Eymond's the tobacconists. the National Insurance Dispensary, better known as Banner's the chemist is at No. 62, the very end of the block being the Grapes Inn Public House

Leicester Buildings, on the corner of Byrom Street and Hunter Street in 1952. Next door is the Weights and Measures office and at No. 7, W. Jones & Co. Ltd, printing works.

Byrom Hall - home to the Liverpool City Mission, Next door, the Army & Navy Stores, when they were really the stores and suppliers of overalls, tarpaulins and tents. Next door on the corner of Circus Street, the Dunbar Castle Public House selling Walkers Falstaff Ales.

No 5 Court, Cartwright Place. June 1933 and although the height of summer, this really is a dingy little area. The stone doorsteps are well worn and in a dangerous condition. There is a metal ash bin on the left for the remnants of yesterday's coal fire and bucket to the right used for bringing water into the house. Just visible are the round coal cellar grids in front of the premises.

A view of the rear of houses on Baptist Street and Gerard Street taken from the window of the top back room of No. 7 Gerard Street. Baptist Street ran from Baptist Lane at the rear of Byrom Hall to Bennett Street parallel with Gerard Street for about half its length. By the time this photograph was taken to record the dilapidation of this slum area many of the properties were being earmarked for demolition. A grand rehousing scheme of tenement walk up flats would regenerate the area within the next four years.

No. 46 Christian Street taken on the 6th October 1926 to record the site of the old Adelphi Theatre next door. A makeshift ladder leans against the wall, heaven forbid you should ever try to use it!

Myrtle View on the 5th May 1927 situated behind the brewery on Holly Street which was originally Myrtle Street. The entrance was at the rear of the Myrtle Public House and the street itself was in a dog leg shape.

LIVERPOOL LULLABY
(STAN KELLY)

Oh you are a mucky kid, dirty as a dustbin lid.
When he hears the things you did, you'll get a belt off your dad.
Oh you have your father's nose, so crimson in the dark it glows,
If you're not asleep when the boozers close,
you'll get a belt off your dad.

You look so scruffy lying there, strawberry jam tats in your hair,
Though in the world you haven't a care, while I have got so many.
It's such a struggle every day, living on your father's pay,
The beggar drinks it all away,
and leaves me hardly any.

Oh you are a mucky kid, dirty as a dustbin lid,
When he hears the things you did, you'll get a belt off your dad.
Oh you have your father's face, you're growing up a real hard case,
There's no-one that can take your place,
go fast asleep for your mammy.

Stan Kelly © Heathside Music Limited 1958.

A photograph taken from the back yard of No. 33 Gerard Street in June 1933. The view is loooking into the scullery, which is what might be called a utility room nowadays. There is a puddle on the floor, which may have been caused by a container of liquid being smashed or the washing hanging on a line above. A small boy is being held whilst a sad looking little girl peers at the camera. This washroom scene was common amongst the court dwellings throughout the city during this period. If you were the proud owner of a mangle you would be the envy of the local neighbourhood and might possibly take in some washing for a small fee.

This is the bedroom of No. 5 Byrom Terrace. Taken in June 1933, it was home to two adults and eight children. The paint is peeling from the ceiling, as is the wallpaper from the damp walls. Makeshift cardboard squares replace long lost window panes and the fireplace is blocked off by a wicker basket containing a bundle of ragged clothes. There is a grand desk/bureau at the end of the bed, the bedstead being of a kind that remarkably is still in fashion today. There is a mishmash of pictures on the walls ranging from cottage and farm scenes to a winged angel.

A photograph of the middle bedroom in an Eldon Street dwelling in 1910. What Laurence Llewelyn Bowen or Linda Barker could do with this room. It is in a very poor condition. The plaster on the wall is falling off to the point that you can see the inside slatting structure of the wall. There is a bed with some ragged clothes draped over the rather grand metal bedstead.

November 1933 and a photograph of 84-88 Gerard Street and 1-11 Whale Street. With December just three weeks away, you are invited to join Lovell's Christmas Club, though that seems the last thing on the minds of the men folk gathered next door. Watch out for the dodgy step or somebody will be putting an injury claim in. Looking up Whale Street you can just see the sign for Lionel Street. (on the far right of the photograph).

18-28 Lionel Street. As the numbers would indicate, there are only six dwellings here but you will note that there are seven arched entrances. The middle one is actually an entry leading through to a number of inner courts. This property jutting out at the bottom of the street is the rear end of the Friends Meeting House which fronted onto Hunter Street.

Nos 18 and 19 Hunter Grove looking north towards Gerard Street in November 1933. Damp proof coursing was non-existent when these four storey dwellings were built. Already there is evidence of a metal plate on the outside wall meaning there is a tie beam in situ to correct a bowing wall. The street runs down a slope making the height of the windowsill of No. 19 markedly higher than that of next door. At the foot of the street there are two cast iron ribbed bollards near to which is parked a handcart.

Gerard Street in February 1933, showing Bennett Street off to the right. The property on the corner was previously the Duck House pub and then Santangeli's ice cream makers, whilst on the opposite corner, Charles Clifton ran a small shop. The shops just visible at the bottom are on Byrom Street, Roberts' is the white building.

1933. Nos 35-51 Hunter Street on its north side just beyond the Friends Meeting House. These are cellar properties and each doorway has a rather posh, albeit flat portico. The buildings generally are of a rickety nature but have been standing for over 100 years. No 35 is showing the work of one of the earliest graffiti artists. You will notice the arm attached to the lamp post which enabled the lamplighter's ladder to lean against it.

1933. Nos 53-75 Hunter Street as a continuation of the last photograph. Viewed here at its junction with Christian Street showing Nos 21-27. Essom & Granell upholsterers are on the corner. Four years later this location would look rather different.

As shiny as a brand new penny. This is the 1937 view of the last scene. Gerard Gardens is now complete and Herbert Tyson Smith's sculptures commissioned by Sir Lancelot Keay take pride of place above the entrances to the square. Old property is still present along Christian Street, lasting until the early 1940s. Notice the gas lamp on Hunter Street and the lamp standard near the main arch are the same ones as on the 1933 Photograph.

1933. No's 21-27 Christian Street from the bottom of Springfield Street looking down Gerard Street. This is the same block as the previous two photographs but looking to the south. There is a tobacconist at the top of Hunter Street advertising Players Weights and Navy Cut cigarettes as well as Brooke Bond Tea amongst others. Part of the property on Christian Street had been demolished and there is a handcart outside Cropper's store. Cameo tobacconists are advertising Will's Woodbines and Star cigarettes but the real deal can be found at Lunt's who are advertising their 'Reductions on prices'

The entrance to the Old Friends Meeting House at 33 Hunter Street. In here, friends could meet for a chat and a cuppa, a piano singalong or to play table tennis or dominoes. It was earmarked for demolition to allow the continuation of Gerard Crescent, which can be seen in the background. However after the air raids of 1941, it was demolished the following year slightly ahead of schedule. This site lay as wasteland for another three years whilst building was halted during the war.

The New Friends Meeting House on the corner of Hunter Street and Mill Lane was built in 1942 to replace the old one which was a little further down Hunter Street on the opposite side. It is pictured here in May 1966. Notice the Zodiac/Zephyr Police car, the type of which would feature in a new T.V. Police series called Z Cars, set in Kirkby, but given the imaginary name of 'Newtown'. At 8pm each Wednesday, the Z car would roll up to the sounds of the pipes and drums of the signature theme tune of 'Johnny Todd', incidentally, the tune to which Everton Football team, and Watford F.C. take to the pitch.

HANGIN' ROUND
(G. FAGAN)

Standing on the stairwell of Gerard Gardens at half past eight,
Snorkel pulled up, hands gloved in wool, for two more friends we wait,
Along the landing they stroll our way, kicking toes to keep out the cold,
The square's deserted on this November night, it's minus two I'm told.

Recalling the day's events we laugh, as plans are made for tomorrow,
Someone suggests we take a walk as another asks to borrow,
As it's off to the chippy under Fonney Oy for nice hot chips and gravy,
Laughing, joking in the shop and banter with the lady.

We take a detour past Hunter Street, heading into town,
It's bitter cold, my nose so red, look like Coco the clown,
Walking past the Museum, in sight the three giant steps,
Lime Street's looking busy, at the column we take a rest.

Guessing the next car colour as they head down London Road,
We're facing Commutation Row, this block is looking old,
The winds sweeps in from Islington so off home we decide to go,
Heading for the subway, walking down the slope, so low.

An internal view of Gerard Gardens, showing the children's playground. High level lighting, railing enclosures and trees and shrubs are all contained within, but were only to last for half of the tenement's life span

Emerging at the other side, we head into the square,
We greet someone we know, who is meeting someone there,
As my fingers numb, turn the front door key - frost bite !
ears feeling just like ice, as we bid each other goodnight.

Gerard Crescent viewed from the recently demolished Old Friends Meeting House in 1945. The Myrtle Public House and Holly Street tenements can be seen in the distance. The three blocks to the left are from top to bottom, Thurlow House, Downe House and Lionel House. Cartwright House is out of the picture.

Another view of Gerard Crescent in 1945 from the brow in front of Cartwright House. The unfinished portion of Gerard Crescent can be seen at close quarters as can part of the rear of Gerard Gardens across the 'backie'. The landings were capped to allow residents to move in ahead of completion.

THE WAY IT WAS
(G. FAGAN)

Hillman Avengers, Minxs and Imps,
A Morris Marina, so old that it limps.
Triumph Toledos, Dolomites and Heralds,
A seventy four N reg to drive at your peril.

The Dandy, the Beano, the Whizzer and Chips,
The Topper with Tiny the big dog were hits.
With Roger the Dodger and Korky the Cat,
And Biffo the Bear, a funny one that.

Cheese cloths and tank tops, 8 button waistbands,
Crepies and parkas for snorkelling on land,
Chelsea boots, kipper ties, knee pocket kecks,
Harrington jackets and high polo necks.

White chewy Pacers were once Opal Mints,
Bulls eyes and Walkers, a Cadbury's Bar Six.
Spangles, Pink Panthers and Bazooka Joes,
Pear drops and humbugs and a bag of Mojos.

The radiogram, wireless, the Granada T.V.
Makes such as D.E.R. push button 3,
Betamax videos, top loading machines,
Soda Stream jet drinks and bags made of beans.

'Not in front of the children' said she,
On the other side, Randall and Hopkirk deceased.
'Til Death us do Part, the Avengers and Skippy,
Emergency Ward 10 or Marcus Welby M.D.

Counting car colours or number plate spotting,
Hide n' seek, football or plain window shopping.
Kick the can, tick, marbles, British Bulldog,
Hopscotch and gutters or playing leapfrog.

Islington Place off Christian Street in 1966. Hyman's wholesale clothing and footwear depot is on the left with the warning 'No Parking opposite this gate'. A happy customer is just leaving John Gianelli's fish and chip shop complete with his Echo wrapped dinner. At the top of Islington Place you can see the rear of the County Sessions House and the side of the Walker Art Gallery.

Gerard Crescent in 1950. The purpose of this photograph was to record the newly installed lifts. Their service did not last too long before they were tinned up. The portion of the Crescent visible to the right of the lift shaft is only a couple of years old itself. When both ends of Gerard Crescent were completed, it contained the longest unbroken run of landings anywhere in Liverpool.

Newly opened Gerard Close in 1952. As it is situated on higher ground than Cartwright House (in the background), it gives the impression of being just as tall a building. However, by 1950, the Council's housing policies had changed to that of three storey flats. As you can see here, each entrance served just six flats, each with a long corridor or hallway, which led from the front door down to the living room with toilet, bathroom and kitchen off to one side, whilst bedrooms led off from the other.

Gerard Gardens 1966.

Gerard Gardens in 1967. The metal stumps around the perimeter of the square are the only · reminder of the playground area which was surrounded by railings.

A panoramic view taken from a back veranda of Gerard Gardens from over the main arch looking across Christian Street. Far left is Clare Street wash house with the rear of old property on St. Anne Street and the chimneys of the four squares visible beyond. The Owen Owen storage warehouse comes next, then the lodging houses on the corner of Springfield, with SFX Spire in the distance. The south side of Springfield Street is mainly taken up by Christ Church School (later, St. Anne's.) The side of Jimmy Romeo's shop can be seen on the corner of Clare Street and the rear of the original Clare's billiards shop on this side of St Anne's Street, Holy Trinity Church standing facing. Back on Christian Street and the property that the bus is going past is the T&GWU building, known as Transport House. The tower of T. J. Hughes building on Stafford Street/London Road can be seen in the middle distance. The rendered gable end of John Gianelli's chip shop is facing us as we pan around to the right. To the rear of this property are the gates and railings to the churchyard of Christ Church, which stood here from 1797 to 1920, the Church having been funded by distiller, John Houghton of the Bull Inn, Trueman Street. You can see the backs of property in Islington including that of Hyman's Wholesale Clothing, Casson's Public House (The Wellington), Clare's Billiards warehouse and Rushworth's Piano stores.

TENNY LIVING
(G. FAGAN)

Amber bubble glass front doors,
Washing lines to hang your smalls,
Rubbish chutes that won't close shut,
Coal holes full with slack and soot.

Lift shafts that have hardly worked,
Stairs of stone all caked in dirt,
Hand carts parked between the yards,
Coal fires covered with their guards,

Tenny living wasn't bad,
It's all some people ever had,
Snug behind your own front door,
It's better than they had before.

A table spread to celebrate the Consecration of the Metropolitan Cathedral of Christ the King on the feast of Pentecost, 14th May 1967. Again, the 'backie' of Gerard Close is used, as it was for 1st Holy Communion celebrations a year later.

Four 'Bottom enders' pictured in May 1974, decked out in their team colours as Liverpool thrash super Macs Newcastle United 3-0 in the F.A. Cup final at Wembley. The location for this photo is the 'backie' of Gerard Close. Bottom enders is actually a term of endearment coined by us Top enders and is not a slight on their preferences in any way, shape or form. My solicitor suggested this disclaimer.

Newly built Holly Street dwellings in 1914, viewed here from Christian Street

Holly Street tenements dating from 1923 are tinned up and condemned to demolition in 1968. This was to make way for the new Saint Anne Street police headquarters, which was to replace the Bridewell in nearby Rose Hill.

The Myrtle Vaults Public House on fire during the demolition of Holly Street tenements at the end of the 1960s

Berry's Pawn Shop at 53 Richmond Row in 1955. One of the last remaining buildings on the stretch from Christian Street to Scotland Place though it was to last until the late 60s

One last remaining resident on Lionel House sees out its last few weeks.

Gerard Gardens 1986. With less than a year remaining, some of the flats are already boarded up.

Tinned up and ready for the crane. Gerard Crescent viewed from the first landing of Lional House with the brew and the Holy Block in the background 1985.

Cartwright House bites the dust in the 1st phase of the Gerard Gardens/Gerard Crescent demolition programme.

An aerial view taken in 1986. Fontenoy Gardens is still going strong, notice the large circle of bonfire damage in the centre of the square. Demolition has started on Cartwright House and new housing to accommodate the families from Gerard Gardens and Gerard Crescent goes up on Comus Street. Across Saint Anne Street, the four squares have long since gone, the space being harshly landscaped including a caged concrete football pitch. Lots of new housing, built under Derek Hatton's Labour Council directive are present on the south side of William Henry Street, taken up by the former residents of Soho Street. The Piggeries still stand for a few more years and Gleave Square is still intact beyond the Radcliffe estate, whilst in the distance are the three blocks of Sheil Park. To the north, John F. Kennedy Heights are on one side of Everton Brow whilst Prince Edwin Walk flats are on the other side. Further along Netherfield Road are Mazzini, Garibaldi and Cavour Heights, George's heights and the Braddocks whilst down off Great Homer Street are the flats on Arkwright Street.

Holy Trinity Church, Saint Anne Street. Seen here in October 1955 from Wilton Street.

Holy Trinity Church under demolition in June 1969 after fire damage.

THE SOHO STREET AREA

Between 1928 and 1931, with the slum clearance programme well underway, Liverpool Corporation entered into the compulsory purchase of commercial property in the Queen Anne Street area between Saint Anne Street and Soho Street. This was to enable an improvement scheme that would rid the area of most of the oldest slum property and tiniest courts in existence to the north side of Islington.

The local population had been served by and large by Holy Trinity Church, Saint Anne Street since its consecration in 1792 (St. Mary of the Angels, known locally as the Friary coming some 118 years later in 1910). The graveyard belonging to the church closed exactly 100 years later in 1892. Holy Trinity would see quite a number of changes throughout the district before its closure in 1968. During the May blitz bombing of 1941 it was badly damaged but was restored and rededicated in 1950. Twice it caught fire, once in 1902, the second time in 1969 causing enough damage to warrant its demolition. Saint Francis Xavier Roman Catholic chapel in nearby Salisbury Street had opened for services on New Years Eve 1847, the magnificent church being erected three years later.

The city planners decided that Torbock Street, Johnson Place, Back Queen Anne Street, Gomer Street, Harker Place, Dickinson Terrace and Travers Street and their incorporated courts would be demolished in their entirety. This would create an oblong site for re-housing, the boundaries being Springfield, Soho Street, Mansfield Street and Wakefield Street with its continuation Harker Street.

Many lodging houses existed on Saint Anne Street, Mansfield Street and Springfield, many of them starting life as Merchant Houses and Ship-owners mansions. This was one of the most fashionable residential areas in the whole of Liverpool in the early 1800s. With the onset of slum dwellings and courts encroaching into the area, the

The junction of St Anne Street with Springfield showing the derelict Wellington Public House and adjoining lodging houses. E. A Clare, Billiards and Bowls suppliers once used Bushell's building as a warehouse. This picture was taken in February 2005.

more affluent of society decided to move out of the area altogether into the south end of the city. Some lodging houses on Springfield (which also ran westwards across Saint Anne Street to Christian Street) still exist to this day, albeit in a derelict state.

After the mass clearance in the early 1930s, four squares of tenements would be created, (hence their local nickname), two on the north side of Queen Anne Street, which would still exist as a through road and two to its south side. The block situated on the corner of Soho Street and Mansfield Street would house a row of shops at its ground level that would serve the community together with other local shops on the east side of Soho Street and in nearby William Henry Street.

Gradually, the blocks sprung up as the remaining streets were demolished around them, making way for the whole complex to be completed in 1935, complete with ornamental designs to the gable ends and stone pot attachments to the roofs.

Saint Mary of the Angels, better known as the Friary, seen here from Everton Brow at its junction with Soho Street. The lone property is M&A Services Auto Repairs at 181 Everton Brow which was once flanked by Railton's tobacconists, Kits Chippy and Joe Mitchell's workshop.

The Church of St. Mary of the Angels in nearby Fox Street, as previously mentioned, was built in 1910 so was relatively new to the new residents of the four squares, though many had come from the surrounding areas. The Church was built on the former site of

Richmond Fair, which had sold Yorkshire Woollen goods from 1787 to 1875.

It was built for the Franciscan Order, funded by Amy Elizabeth Imrie who was the heiress to the famous White Star Line Shipping Co., which built the ill fated Titanic. Run by the Franciscan Monks, it quickly became known as the Friary. The Church contains many Italian artefacts, brought over from Italy at the insistence of Amy

The old and the new. Insanitary property in Torbock, Gomer and Travers Street were cleared for a grand rehousing scheme that was to be known locally as the Four Squares. Shown here are the blocks near Queen Anne Street.

Elizabeth including the statues of St. Francis, St. Anthony, St. Elizabeth and St. Clare, which were designed by Professor Carisi of Rome.

The Cipollino columns and coloured marble altar are of the rarest kind and the balustrade of alabaster and the pavement of the sanctuary formerly belonged to the Church of St. Nicholas in Carcere in Rome and are regarded as relics of the Eternal City. The imposing high altar is of the style that belongs to the 16th Century and originally stood in Bologna Cathedral, having been dedicated to St. Anne. A

Queen Anne Place in 1933. Such a grand name was deserving of a ultra-modern development, complete with ornamantal pots and railings.

replica oil painting of Perugino's 'Our lady of the angels' also adorns the Church, the original being located in the famous gallery of Bologna.

The front altar, originally the Church pulpit, is composed of antique marble in a Roman Gothic design, the like of which is rarely seen outside Italy. It is documented that St. Ignatius of Loyola, St. Philip Neri and St. Charles Borrommeo have preached from this pulpit and offered up High Mass at the High Altar in St. Mary of the Angels.

1933. Part of the Four Squares Complex seen from the junction of Wakefield Street and Mansfield Street. On the left we look east along Mansfield Street and beyond Soho Street to William Henry Street. To the right we look along Wakefield Street and across Queen Anne Street to Harker Street.

In 1979 the Franciscans gave the church to the Catholic Archdiocese of Liverpool but due to a dwindling congregation, possibly because of the falling housing stock within the area, the church closed in December 2001 as part of the 'pastoral regeneration'. A Grade II listing will thankfully protect the church from the fate suffered by the nearby parishes of St. Joseph's in 1979 and Holy Cross in 2003, both of whom lost their churches to the bulldozer.

Even so, it is a shame that a building of such architectural beauty that has meant so much to so many over the last 95 years is lying idle. To this end, a campaign has been running, headed by local figure, Kay Kelly to secure hopefully, the resurgence of the Friary.

SCOTLAND ROAD

A 1958 view across Scotland Place and up Scotland Road. The rear of the Birmingham Arms Public House is looking old and tired and is seeing out its last few years as a drinking establishment on Richmond Row. The public conveniences are still present in Scotland Place facing Fontenoy Gardens and Melia's shop can be seen on the corner of Addison Street. The site here is earmarked for the new Technical College.

Saint Anthony's Church was first established by a French refugee priest, Father Jean Baptiste Antoine Gerardot in 1804. Situated near to the junction of Dryden Street and Scotland Road, widening of the thoroughfare and a growing congregation meant it was relocated to its present site in 1833 where a more lavish Gothic structure was designed. Father Newsham founded St. Anthony's School in Newsham Street in 1844.

In the mid 1800s the Silvester Street area was awash with Irish immigrants who had managed to flee the potato famine. Such was this containment in such a small area, that there was a requirement for another school and a church. In 1874 St. Sylvester's school opened as a result of the Education Act, which had come into being at the beginning of 1870. Plans were proposed for the building of an accompanying church, masses having been previously taken at a nearby shed and now in the school itself. In 1889 St. Sylvester's Church, built of red brick in a Gothic style was consecrated and opened for worship. In 1911, a new school was constructed on the corner of Latimer Street and this was opened four years later by Archbishop Whiteside.

The Vauxhall and Scotland Road area is steeped in history when it comes to the pioneering of municipal housing for the poor, the likes of which had never been seen before. The Liverpool Sanitary Amendment Act was introduced in 1864, quickly followed by the

Chaucer House 1936. These were situated on the junction of Scotland Road and Juvenal Street almost opposite Victoria Square. Note the line of the floor level within the flats as Scotland Road falls away to the right. Nash Grove can be seen just behind.

Labouring Classes Dwelling House Act two years later. This signalled the go ahead for court dwellings and cellar property to be cleared in the Silvester Street and Ashfield Street area to make way for the first municipal housing to be built in the whole of Europe.

St. Martin's Cottages were opened in 1869. Hardly cottages as we know them, they comprised six blocks of four storey tenements built in an E shape with a mirror image directly opposite. The 124 flats ranged from 1 to 3 bedroom dwellings with a living room and scullery. They were lit by gas with cooking over an open fire. There were no bathrooms and the toilets were communal on half landings until modernisation in the 1950s.

A decade later and approaching 100 years old, moves were made to ensure that the cottages were preserved as a monument to innovative housing. Alas, they were only to last a further decade before the decision was taken to demolish them in 1977. A commemorative

plaque takes pride of place within the Silvestrian Sports and Social club complex in Silvester Street.

It was to be another sixteen years in 1885 before the City Corporation embarked on a second development of low cost municipal housing. These being the Victoria Square settlement which replaced the slum property in and

1966. Cazneau Street. named after Joseph Cazneau, a Merchant who built his house here in 1796. This view is looking south towards St Anne's Church on St Anne Street from the corner of Horatio Street. St Martin's Market is on the left, the Denbigh Castle Public House is jutting out on the right near to the junction with Juvenal Street

around Juvenal Street and Lawrence Street on the east side of Scotland Road.

These comprised 269 flats and 12 shops, built in a quadrangle around a central square. Varying from a single room to 3 bedrooms, two flats would share a toilet with sinks provided on each landing. This

1966. another view of 'Paddy's Market' at the junction with Juvenal Street looking east towards Great Homer Street. The Clock Hotel Public House, listed as 36 Cazneau Street and 36 Juvenal Street is on the opposite corner.

development won an architectural award for their advanced design when erected, such was their splendour as to what had gone before. One of the blocks was severely damaged during the May blitz of 1941 and subsequently demolished. The remaining blocks succumbed to the demolition enveloping the area in 1966 to make way for the entrance to the Kingsway Mersey Tunnel, which was opened in 1971.

A third, smaller development called Juvenal Buildings was constructed opposite Victoria Square on the south side of Juvenal Street in 1890.

GOODBYE SCOTTIE ROAD
(T. Baines)

The years have passed since my last abode,
Was Dryden Street in old Scottie Road.
Times have changed since I was there,
No Chiappes café, no Vicky Square.

There's no Rotunda, no Champion Whates,
No Paddy's Market, no Mary Kates
The Gaiety's gone, the Derby too,
And those Mary Ellens are very few.

Even the scuffer on the beat,
No longer walks the lonely street.
Once there were people with smiling faces,
Now there's nothing but dust and empty spaces.

Once there were lamplighters, who lit the gas,
While people were hurrying off to mass.
In the summer the women would sit chatting on steps,
While bookies runners stood taking the bets.

Now Sunday football was played in the street
And saltfish for breakfast was quite a treat.
We had fresh necks, spare ribs and thick barley soup
And pans full of scouse what the old-girl cooked.

Somebody must have had a 'job lot' on Mini Coopers in 1966 judging by this view up Scotland Road near to its junction with Bevington Hill. Loyd's Ward's and Shelton's flank Cousin's bakery shop and the round Counter café is at the end of the block.

Now 'full coe' was the cry of the kids in our street,
When they'd see their mates with something to eat.
And that lolly-ice man on his threewheeler bike,
Was always a nap to get into a fight.

Now there was a man with a birdcage with an apple inside,
He swore he had two but the other one died,
And there was old Janey Swain who was very well known,
Because she was alright if you needed a loan.

There was old Jimmy Gunnion a barber by trade
And old Mary Blunne who sold a good fade.
There was Nelly and Josie, the Ensor twins,
And Harry the muckman who worked on the bins.

There was old Johnnie Wallace who'd stand squeezing his plums
'all fresh this morning' he belch from his lungs.
And 'heads-a-dollar' was another old cry,
As the dockers tossed ha'pennies up to the sky.

'Exy Echo Final' was another sound heard,
from the newspaper lad, these were well known words.
And 'jam jars or rags' you could hear someone cry,
As the ragman with handcart, slowly walked by.

And the hooves of Dodds horses on cobblestones rang,
While in the distance a busker sang.
Now lallio and rounders were the games played by kids,
And your ma and your da would join in for kicks.

Now there were three famous shops where you could pawn gear,
these were Cookson's, Stanley's and old Jim O'Hares.
There was a scoff house called Thorns where you could have a sly kip
After your two college puddings and your big bowl of thick.

Now Telford's the sweet shop was just facing Thorns,
Where peardrops, caramels and chocolate buttons were bought.
Clarkson's by the library, was the biggest shop on the road,
Where you could buy clothing and items untold.

There was the wash-house where women fought for a mangle,
And after the fight they would have a good jangle.
There was the Morning Star pub where the Irishmen lurked,
While over a pint they'd talk about work.

Now the tramcars ran along old Scottie Road
And believe me, in winter, inside they were cold.
They passed Saint Anthony's Church, which is still standing there,
The only church on the road where you could say a prayer.

Now here's some famous boxers who to watch was a joy.
Volante, Gannon, Butcher, Tommy and Jimmy Molloy.
And here's some famous soccer stars I must give credit to,
Morrisey, Tansey, Melia, Campbell and the Gannons two !

Yes, these are only memories now of my last abode,
Memories of my younger days in good old Scottie Road.
So it's 'goodbye Scottie Road' old friend we'll never meet again,
For even though you're being rebuilt, you'll never be the same.

GAS LAMPS DOWN SCOTTIE
(J. Gilfoyle)

Connie onnie butties, Spam and salt fish
Memories of mine and dreams that I miss.
Scouse on a Monday, that great Irish stew,
I remember it all - do you ?

Woodstock Gardens in the Silvester Street and Westmoreland Place area. Built together with Hopwood and Ashfield Gardens as a housing improvement scheme in the 1930s, they lasted until 1984.

Gas lamps down Scottie, I remember those nights
Ice cold and frosty, flickering gas lights
All snug in a bed, my family and me
The wind blowing so cold, in from the sea.

The ships on the river, we could barely hear
As they sounded their foghorns, to keep other ships clear
The wind shook our windows in our tenement flat
With gas lamps down Scottie, I remember all that.

Queues at the gasworks, waiting for coke,
Just half a bag please, my mother's flat broke,
Shivering with cold, waiting your turn,
The family all waiting for something to burn.

And so back home, a fire to light
All nice and cosy, as down came the night
Frost on the windows and snow on the sill,
I remember those times and I always will.

Scottie Road looking north. There are no road markings so just go where you want. Wilbraham House tenements can be seen on the right.

A 1964 aerial view of the Vauxhall area. Wilbraham House is situated top right of the photograph, just south of Saint Anthony's Church. The tenement flats mentioned on Westmoreland Place take up most of the Scotland Road population facing Saint Anthony's. Archbishop Whiteside school and St. Martin's cottages can be seen on Silvester Street whilst further north, St. Gerard's is on Boundary Street, which was the old boundary with Kirkdale. Hopwood Street divides the 1930s tenements from the later three storey flats, which are just over a decade old. At the bottom of the photograph is the industry, which existed alongside the Liverpool/Leeds canal including Athol Street Gasworks.

An era that's gone and will never return,
Parents were loving but ever so stern.
The kids all scrubbed, cleaned and fed
Dripping butties and cocoa, then off to bed.

With great coats for blankets and six of us to a bed,
Feet at the bottom, by my brother's head
All lovely memories I'll take to my grave,
Of friends that I knew, whose memories I'll save

Of times that have passed, the good and the bad,
Yes I remember old Scottie, when I was a lad.

Hopwood Street looking towards Scotland Road. This was part of the new housing scheme in the area. Benledi Street, built in a similar fashion, backs onto these.

In the early 1900s Scotland Road was famous for having over 220 Public Houses in its immediate vicinity with over 60 on the actual road itself. These establishments were famous for their characters who varied from story tellers and singers to children and men folk well

Above: Victoria Square central courtyard. The four buildings in the centre are air raid shelters that were built during World War II.

Below: 1944, showing blitz damage suffered three years earlier.

versed in the art of giving poetry recitals. The bleak depression of the 1930s saw a heavy decline in the number of Public Houses until the numbers were halved by the 1950s. The biggest single disaster to befall this community was the mass clearance programme of the 1950s and 1960s, particularly affecting the stretch from Addison Street to Dryden Street, which was demolished to make way for the Kingsway tunnel approach road. Presently, only 3 Public Houses currently survive on Scotland Road, these being, The Throstles' Nest, The Eagle Vaults on the east side and The Parrot on the west side.

In 1923, the City of Liverpool Corporation placed an application for an order confirming a scheme under the Housing of the Working Classes Acts of 1890 to 1921. Plans were presented to improve the areas specific to Burlington Street, Hopwood Street, Great Richmond Street and Rankin Street. The tenement blocks of Woodstock, Ashfield and Hopwood Gardens were born out of this scheme, completed in 1938 they were demolished less than 50 years later in 1983/84.

VAUXHALL ROAD

Vauxhall Road in 1966, showing the Vauxhall vaults, (known locally as Dangster's), on the corner of Cockspur Street. Vauxhall Gardens are just in view and the John Moores College is being built.

Highfield Street from Leeds Street in 1967. On the left are the offices of William Costigans grocers. On the right, Tetley's are making a delivery of ale to the Coach and Horses. Highfield Garden's tenements can be seen in the background.

A 1967 north view of Vauxhall Road looking past the Eagle Vaults from Blackstock Street. Fairries & Co. Sugar refiners, part of the Tate & Lyle industry can be seen.

BACK BUCHANAN STREET
(Harry & George Dison)

A fella from the corpy, just out of planning school,
Has told us that we've got to move, right out of Liverpool.
They're moving us to Kirkby, to Skelmersdale or Speke,
But we wanna stay where we used to play in Back Buchanan Street.

Don't wanna go to Kirkby, don't wanna go to Speke,
Don't wanna go from all we know in Back Buchanan Street.

I'll miss the corner pub with the parlour painted red,
Likewise the green goddesses, likewise the overhead,
And lots of other things like putting out the cat,
Cos there's no back door on the 14th floor of a corpy tower flat.

I'll miss the Mary Ellens, me dad'll miss the docks,
Me gran'll miss the wash-house where she washed me grandad's socks,
They've pulled down Paddy's Market where me ma once had a stall,
And soon their picks and shovels will be through our backyard wall.

Don't wanna go to Kirkby, don't wanna go to Speke,
Don't wanna go from all I know in Back Buchanan street.

From Bootle to the Dingle, you can hear the same old cry,
Stop mucking round with Liverpool, at least until I die.

Blackstock Gardens under construction in early 1934. Morris's Plumbers & Decorators of Colquitt Street, Liverpool proudly display their sign. Bricks with a light facing finish were used here, very similar to Great Richmond Street dwellings of a decade earlier. Note, that where Pegram's Stores is to be built, brickwork with an ordinary finish was used as it was no good wasting 'good' expensive bricks where they were not to be seen. Breeze blocks are used in similar situations in this day and age. The block was completed in June 1934.

Blackstock Gardens central square in 1934

Blackstock Gardens seen here from Paul Street in 1934.

Between 1902 and 1905, the Liverpool City Engineer's Department took over 100 photographs concerning the planning, construction and completion of another ground breaking method of building, this time involving a substance known as clinker.

Clinker is the residue of having burnt rubbish in a refuse destructor, something the City Corporation had started to do. The mixture would then be placed into moulds to make concrete walls, floors and ceilings. This all took place at Cobbs Quarry in St. Domingo Road, Liverpool 5 and would then be delivered to site on steam traction engines pulling a trailer. The site for the construction of this block of flats would be Eldon Street off Vauxhall Road.

7/5/1904. The front view of the foundations going in for the innovative flats on Eldon Street. The rear of the old property on neighbouring streets can be seen.

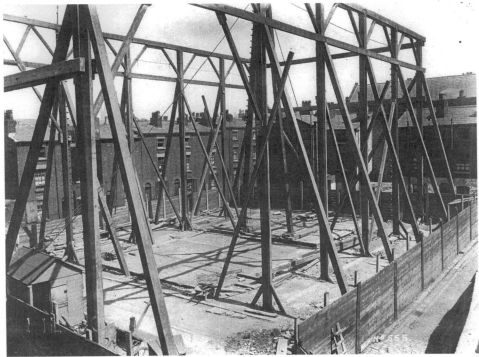

30/8/1904. The rear view of the newly erected timber frame from within which the flats were built. Eldon Street terracing can be seen opposite.

A steam driven traction engine full of the pre-fabricated concrete slabs is seen leaving Cobbs Quarry on St. Domingo Road, Everton.

Pioneered by Liverpool City Engineer, John Brodie, first a prototype house made of these prefabricated slabs would be assembled at Cobbs Quarry to test the feasibility of such a project. A testing floor was present at the quarry as was a timber frame, steel girders and a pulley with hoist, all of which would be transported to the site at Eldon Street to enable the safe construction of the flats.

2/9/1904. Upon arrival on site, workmen would climb a ladder and fix the crane hook to the slab and position it in place straight from the wagon.

2/9/1904. Timbers hold the slabs upright whilst they set. Another slab is on a winch and is being guided by some workmen.

14/9/1904. Showing the development's progress from the back of property on Vauxhall Road. The Church of Our Lady of Reconciliation can just be seen top right.

20/9/1904. No. 1 staircase is in place whilst an ornate pillar is leaning against the timber frame waiting to be installed.

The foundations were laid in May 1904, the first residents having moved in within a year. The cost of the development was estimated to have been only half as much as that of traditional construction methods. For one reason or another, no more were built in Liverpool though the method did lend a hand in the way the Royal Liver Buildings were built using slabs of reinforced concrete and granite cladding four years later, one of the first buildings in the world to do so.

17/11/1904. Already the upper floor is taking shape. Four men work the winch from a gantry, which runs on wheels along a timber frame.

9/2/1905. The ornate cornice is in place and a workman is painting the railings.

Eldon Street dwellings were innovative also in design. With sealed floors of concrete containing a curved skirting from wall to floor, it meant that floors could be swilled clean without fear of seeping water through floorboards. The rear balconies housed an enclosed toilet and a rubbish chute linked the balconies vertically with a door at the ground level to enable collection of the rubbish by the refuse wagon. Metal railings, carved internal pillars and ornate external cornices and balconies completed a pleasant aesthetic look to the building. Sadly, although

14/2/1905. In this rear view, there is a hive of activity as workmen cement the roof and add doors. Chimneys are visible in the distance, which belong to one of the many tanneries on Vauxhall Road.

touted as a unique vision for the future as no doubt they were at the time, the block was demolished in the 1960s, the land being used for the building of the new Our Lady of Reconciliation School now renamed Trinity School. The caretaker's bungalow belonging to the school actually sits directly on the site of the flats.

19/4/1905. The site is now cleared as a mother and child survey the scene. Curtains hang in a few of the windows whilst a first floor flat asks 'to be let'.

19/4/1905. The completed rear view, showing balconies with an enclosed toilet and rubbish chute.

WHISKY ON A SUNDAY (SETH DAVY)
(G. Hughes)

He sat on the corner of Bevington Bush,
on top of an old packing case,
He had three wooden dolls that could dance and could sing,
And he crooned with a smile on his face.

Come day, go day, wish in me heart it was Sunday,
Drinking buttermilk through the week, Whisky on a Sunday.

His tired old hands tugged away at the strings, and the puppets,
they danced up and down.
A far better show than you ever would see,
at the Tatler or Gayo in town.

Come day, go day, wish in me heart it was Sunday,
Drinking buttermilk through the week, Whisky on a Sunday.

In nineteen o'five, old Seth Davy died,
and his song was heard no-more,
The three dancing dolls ended up in the bin
and the plank went to mend a back door.

Come day, go day, wish in me heart it was Sunday,
Drinking buttermilk all the week, Whisky on a Sunday.

On some stormy nights, down Scottie Road way,
when the wind's blowing up from the sea.
You can still hear the song that old Seth Davy sang,
as he crooned to his dancing dolls three.

Come day, go day, wish in me heart it was Sunday,
Drinking buttermilk all the week, Whisky on a Sunday.

Two views of Silvester Street on 8th April 1924. Viewing the south side looking west towards Vauxhall Road. A number of terraces branch off on the left towards courts. St. Martin's walled recreation ground is beyond St. Augustine Street. The Church of St. Martin-in-the-field, known locally as the 'Black Church' is also pictured. It was so called because of the volumes of sulphurous smoke that had enveloped it, originating from a nearby soda manufacturers owned by Irishman, James Muspratt. The foundation stone of the Church was laid in 1825 and was described as being built from the elegant design of Mr. John Foster. It was further described as being a large and handsome stone church erected on a piece of land situated on the south side of a certain street called Great Oxford Street and Oxford Street North which was renamed Silvester Street in 1865. It was consecrated on 13th January 1829 but succumbed to enemy action in 1941, closing permanently for services in May 1949.

Silvester Street North side some forty years later on 29th March 1967. Woodstock Gardens are now in view.

Burlington Street, tenements. Looking west towards Vauxhall Road. Tarmacadam is being laid in front of what will become the ground floor shops

Left: St. Martin's Cottages seen from the corner of Vauxhall Road and Ashfield Street in 1967.

Below: The same view a decade later whilst under demolition. You'll notice that Ford Cortina Mk III owners were real hard cases, taking no heed of the danger warnings present.

AN ODE TO THE DECADE OF THE SUPER 70s
(G. Fagan)

1970

The Beatles, Supremes, Simon & Garfunkel are no more,
The Mexico world cup, the Brazilians pure football.
The Chopper bike and Rolf's Stylophone hit the shops with force,
The Clangers and Scooby-Doo and the film, 'Kes' of course.
The car of the day is the Triumph, in deluxe and four doors,
The mini, midi and maxi skirts are 'all the go' in stores.
Opportunity knocked for Dana as the Charlies fought the war,
In the summertime for Mungo Jerry before the drink and drive law.

1971

Give us a twirl said Brucey to Anthea on the Generation Game,
Jackie Stewart and Harvey Smith are the sportsmen of the day.
Benny Hill and Clive Dunn then Rod Stewart's Maggie May,
Hot pants and high heeled boots are the fashion so they say.
Chirpy chirpy cheep cheep, knock three times and early Slade,
The Banana splits and space hoppers and there was no E-Bay.
Crossfire and Corgi cars were the boys toys by the way,
The Liver Birds on T.V. and decimal coinage in your pay.

1972

Blue Peter and Magpie tussle it out on your T.V.
I'd like to teach the world to sing in perfect harmony.
Marc Bolan and the Osmonds and David Cassidy,
Action man and roller skates, a pittance licence fee.
Mark Spitz wins seven gold medals at his Munich swimming spree,
Where terrorists strike a blow, against all humanity.
Cabaret is a box office draw with Liza Minelli,
The Harlem globetrotters, are the biggest team to see.

1973

Britain's into Europe but we're hit by power cuts,
Remington shavers and Vymura wallpaper it seems they are a must.

Bruce Lee and Kojak, a lollipop he sucks,
The Austin Allegro is in while Poland knock us out the cup.
The Sweet, Slade and Gary G are riding up the charts,
Live and Let Die is the Bond movie as Roger Moore stars.
Burton and Taylor split as Princess Ann and Mark Phillips wed,
Morecambe and Wise and Mike Yarwood are the T.V. tops with cred.

1974

Kellogg's Super Noodles, Birds Angel Delight and Instant mash,
Vesta chow mein, Slimcea, Nimble bread and corned beef hash.
Pan's People make their debut on this year's top of the pops,
Stardust, Essex, Quatro, Mud and Paper Lace are tops.
Video recorders and ping pong arcade games are in,
LFC make super Mac a loser, as they win.
Roobarb and Custard, the Ford Capri, the car that's fast,
The Wombles and It Ain't Half Hot Mum, T.V. favourites past.

1975

The wrestling on the telly, Jackie Pallo's Tough Tag Team,
Kendo Nagasaki and his forearm smash are mean.
Regan, Carter and the Sweeney and the Fonz in happy days,
Jim'll fix it for you if you write to him today.
The sportsman of the moment is a man called Barry Sheen,
Trophies, speed and metal pins, he rides a mean machine.
Hai Karate, Denim, Brut and Old Spice are for men,
While it's tartan suits and criss cross kilts and five scotch blokes for them.

1976

Donna Summer, Tina Charles and disco fever's near,
But Abba's Dancing Queen, Fernando, Mama Mia's here.
The long hot summer sees the tarmac bubble, boil and pop,
Zoom and Fabs and ice pops, Ninety Nines and R. Whites pop.
Starsky and Hutch hit the screens with their trademark car,
As the Muppet Show with a frog and a pig and Bert and Ernie star.
The Punk rock scene hits London spreading far and wide this year,
While C.B. radios become the 'Yorkie' truckers gear.

1977

The Silver jubilee is the news of seventy seven,
A yank called David Soul charts twice as Elvis goes to heaven.
Take hart, morph and space dust sweets this year all make their bow,
Pot noodles, slime and skateboards are the newest crazes now.
The girls have Jackie and Blue Jeans with problems page and all,
Bodie and Doyle are the professionals, bonjour Chanson d'Amour.
Star wars on the silver screen, Carrie Fisher, Harrison Ford,
God save the Queen sang John Lydon, Kintyre breaks the record.

1978

Space Invaders everywhere, Dean Friedman with his curly hair,
The Hulk, Blakes 7, Wonderwoman,
Kenny Everett's video shows are buzzin'
Grease is the word for Olivia and John,
Buy a Soda Stream jet before they're gone.
Mousetrap, Frustration, Rebound and Simon,
All games to kill for, oh and Sarah Brightman.
Matchstalk men and cats and dogs,
No love thy neighbour - no nig-nogs.
Liverpool retain the Euro pot,
Whilst Boney M take the yule top spot.

1979

Coloured vinyl, picture discs, the Police and Tubeway army hits,
Monkey magic, Cindy dolls, Top Deck shandy, Euro hols.
Dudley Moore, Bo Derek's 10, Y.M.C.A the Village Men,
Stretch denim jeans, Lee Cooper fades,
Pink Floyds wall, leif Garrett's shades.
Two tone, Ska, the new Mod scene,
With Selektor, the Specials and Madness keen.
Alien and the Deer Hunter also showing
The end of a decade ends with it snowing.

NETHERFIELD ROAD

A mid 1960s view of Saint George's Heights on Saint George's Hill which overlooked Netherfield Road at its north/south intersection. The King Edward Hotel public house is seen here at the top of Roscommon Street.

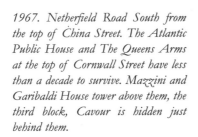

1967. Netherfield Road South from the top of China Street. The Atlantic Public House and The Queens Arms at the top of Cornwall Street have less than a decade to survive. Mazzini and Garibaldi House tower above them, the third block, Cavour is hidden just behind them.

Netherfield Road South in 1966, from the top of Prince Edwin Street. Cresswell Mount high rise flats on Everton Terrace give their residents a good view across the Mersey. The Crescent Public House stands facing at the top of 'Prinny Eddie'.

Sir Thomas White Gardens, Saint Domingo Road in the summer of 1938. Newly erected, it is interesting to note the different designs to the balconies than those built previously. This newer version also features a metal rail. The first floor balcony is not as high as the ones above due to the different mezzanine levels of the flats.

SCENES FROM
WITHIN THE SQUARE

Jumpers for goalposts. The Bullring in 1970. Many a skill was honed in the uncompromising surroundings of tarmac, concrete and glass. There were forever arguments about whether the ball had gone over the 'imaginary crossbar' or over the 'post', and the referee's think they've got it bad nowadays? If you belonged to one of the local boxing clubs, it was most likely that your word was taken as gospel.

DERBY DAY BLUES (OR REDS)
(G. Fagan)

Saturday afternoon, tears of joy or doom and gloom,
At half past two the pubs let out to a shower of red and blue,
Chippys packed around the ground release the fans onto the street,
Whose day will it be, our number nine or a sad defeat.
Depending on your persuasion, rattles and rosettes in your colours,
Team news eagerly awaited as you split away from brothers,

Will St. John score from Hunts Cross, that will surely be a record,
Or will the golden vision visit the Temple having scored.

The years roll on but still it is the game of the season,
Fifty thousand plus crammed in, there seems no rhyme or reason,
Latchford is up front today and Keegan for the reds,
Neither were to ever score in this fixture with foot or head.

The sleeping giant has awoken as Kendall's school of science feast,
Sharp and Inchy, Reid and Bracewell, Gray and Pat the beast,
Fagan's reds in Europe too, the Euro cup comes home,
Hansen, Brucie, Rush and Whelan and memories of Rome.

Bragging rights on Merseyside for the winner of this game,
The Derby's in full swing again, who will be the name,
That everyone will talk about come ten to five tonight,
Four months to wait till your revenge if we don't get it right.

Caryl Gardens children's play area on a sunny Easter Bank Holiday in 1937. Most present here will be octogenarians by now.

SLOW DANCE
(ARR G. FAGAN)

Have you ever watched kids on a merry-go-round?
Or listened to the rain, hitting the ground?
Ever followed a butterfly's erratic flight?
Or gazed at the sun, fading into the night?

You'd better slow down, don't dance so fast,
Time is short, the music won't last.

Do you run through each day, making it fly?
When you ask 'how are you ?, do you hear the reply?
When the day is done, do you lie in your bed,
With the next hundred chores running through your head?

Ever told your child, we'll do it tomorrow?
And in your haste, not see their sorrow?
Ever lost touch, let a good friendship die,
Cos you never had time to call and say 'hi'?

You'd better slow down, don't dance so fast,
Time is short, the music won't last.

Newly built Myrtle Gardens in 1936. these tenements were posh, I mean come on, they had laundry rooms, oh what splendour.

When you run so fast to get somewhere,
You miss half the fun of getting there,
When you worry and scurry and hurry your day,
It's like an unopened gift, just thrown away.

You'd better slow down, don't dance so fast,
Time is short, the music won't last.

Life's not a race, do take it slower,
Hear the music, before the song is over!

A Memorial in Blackstock Gardens.

A procession through Highfield Gardens in 1953 marking the opening of the new Saint Mary's Church in Highfield Street. The original was destroyed during the blitz bombing.

A still shot of local hoodlum Johnny Murphy in Gerard Gardens. The part was played by David McCallum in the film 'The Violent Playground' (Rank 1958)

Stanley Baker and some of the crew and extras take a break from filming 'The Violent Playground' in 1957 (released a year later). The location here is the 'oller' known then as the hills, in the background is the Holy Block which was part of the Gerard Crescent Complex.

Gerard Gardens Kids 1966.

The Women's Football Match. The two teams pose proudly in Gerard Gardens in the mid 1970s.

Warwick Gardens in December 1938 showing some locals posing outside Garrett's general store.

Warwick Gardens viewed from Caryl Gardens

ST. JOEY'S
(G. FAGAN)

Saturday evening, dragged to church.
Confession night, smell the frankincense and myrrh.
Sunday evening, dragged to church.
A one hour mass, seemed to last the earth.
It's only ten years since my birth,
Football and hide n' seek in the square,
Is where I should be - tennis, my serve?

I'm older now and off to church.
The one in my heart, but it's not there.
There's just a big tarmac, where once was my church.
How could they raze it, its meaning, its worth?
I wish I could re-wind, so that I could hear.
The sermons, the hymns, the organ so dear.
There was plenty of time for fun in the square.

Saint Joseph's Church, Grosvenor Street and its Presbytery.

Mersey Memories ©

Gerard Gardens, Liverpool 3, 1976

1a. Harry Mullins
1b. Eileen Gallagher
1c. William Grierson
1d. Elizabeth Dowling
1e. James Ellison
2b. Thomas Sharples
2c. Marion Lindsay
2d. Mary Burns
2e. Robert Patty
3a. William Sutherland
3b. Mary Dowling
3c. Thomas Borrows
3d. Anthony Farrell
4. Sarah Rowan
4a. John Lovett
4b. William Duncan
4c. George Strode
4d. John O'Hara
5. Mary O'Connell
5a. Harriet Ventre
5b. George Bowness
5c. Margaret Lee
5d. Patricia Connoll,
6. Frank Sedgwick
6a. Ellen Mee
6b. Catherine Dalton
6c. Michael Goulding
6d. Elizabeth Allt
7. Michael Gallagher
7a. James Blakemore
7b. Francis Parry
7c. Michael Goulding
7d. Kathleen Wright
8. Bridget Molloy
8a. Cecilia Robinson
8b. Peter Baccino
8c. James Rattigan
8d. Michael Campbell
9. Patrick McHale
9a. Dominic Wiles
9b. Julia Georgeson
9c. John McMullen
9d. George Duncan
10. Margaret Harrison
10a. Anthony D'Annunzio

10b. Veronica D'Annunzio
10c. John Leonard
10d. Thomas Kelly
11. Mary Roberts
11a. Angela Carlyle
11b. Winifred Fields
11c. Anthony Duncan
11d. Edward Blakemore
12. William Fay
12a. Michael Bailey
12b. Margaret Rogan
12c. Gerard Allt
12d. Sarah Clayton
14. Catherine Otty
14a. Christopher Baccino
14b. Ann Jenkins
14c. Thomas Dunne
14d. Richard Pattie
15. George Weetman
15a. Antony Mielo
15b. Catherine McHale
15c. John Bowness
15d. Charles, Gerard, Paul
      & Ann Marie Higgins
16. Bridget Sallery
16a. Veronica Strode
16b. Martin Brady
16c. John McShane
16d. William Edgar
17a. Alfred Keegan
17b. Jane Mullen
17c. Robert Cahill
17d. Thomas Molloy
18. Walter Iles
18a. Annie Francis
18b. Patrick Campbell
18c. Arthur Rothwell
18d. William Healey
19. Elizabeth Bellis
19a. Florence Sallery
19b. Francis Jordan
19c. Mary Jones
19d. Veronica Jones
20. Mary Rathbone
20a. Thomas Peet

20b. Thomas Sweeney
20c. Mary Wrigley
20d. Phyllis Creighton
21. Charles Burke
21a. Mary Ambrose
21b. Bridget Moore
21c. Andrew Shields
21d. Harold McHarron
22. Charles Griffiths
22a. Maria Redhead
22b. Patrick Salkeld
22c. Michael Wright
22d. Kenneth Jones
23. Philip Boffey
23a. James Temple
23b. Catherine McGovern
23c. Peter Healing
23d. Mary Bethel
24. Margaret Walsh
24a. Peter Stanton
24b. James Thompson
24c. Sarah Boffey
24d. Thomas Banks
25. John Porter
25a. Arthur Pullen
25b. Margaret Dunn
25c. Francis Wiles
25d. John Campbell
26. Margaret Kildare
26a. Mary Jones
26b. Joseph Jones
26c. Bridget Blakemore
26d. Michael Ventre
27. Margaret Burke
27a. Mary Parsley
27b. Gerard Duncan
27c. George Smith
27d. Susan Thompson
28. James Richardson
28a. Clara Doherty
28b. Timothy Chesham
28c. Ellen Dixon
28d. John Campbell
29a. Bernard O'Rourke
29b. Peter Stanton
29c. Joseph Lindsay
29d. Aloysius Miello

MERSEY MEMORIES

Gerard Crescent, Liverpool 3, 1974

1. Cornelius Parry
1a. William Riley
1b. Jane Taylor
1c. Maureen McDowell
1d. Philip Kenny
2. Denis Connor
2a. Maria Walker
2b. Arthur Vaughan
2c. Sarah Quinn
2d. Annie Price
3. George Nutter
3a. William Strode
3b. Joseph Lenehan
3c. Peter O'Hara
3d. Patrick Cushing
4. Christopher O'Neill
4a. Mary Lester
4b. Francis Sudbery
4c. Harry Pratt
4d. William Spring
5a. Michael Connor
5b. Walter Rawlins
5c. Winifred Smith
5d. Barbara Goodwin
6. Charles Moore
6a. Edward Fulton
6b. John Culshaw
6c. Aidan Murphy
6d. Kathleen Clark
7. Susan Schorah
7a. Mary Kelly
7b. Richard Jastrzebski
7c. Annie Martin
7d. Primrose Dale

8. Robert Allen
8a. Sarah Parry
8b. John Germain
8c. Francis Donohue
8d. Joseph Murphy
9. John Livingstone
9a. Robert Allen
9b. Alfred Tallon
9c. Thomas Taylor
9d. Charles Birkett
10. Richard Redhead
10a. Margaret Smith
10b. Raymond Baccino
10c. Thomas Macauley
10d. Catherine Gallagher
11. Maria Muscatelli
11a. James Hanratty
11b. James Wafer
11c. Leonard Welch
11d. Elizabeth Crawford
12. Margaret Redmond
12a. Edward Yates
12b. Robert Grierson
12c. Rosina Parry
12d. Margaret Roan
14. Michael Vaughan
14a. John Marshall
14b. George Carter
14c. Kevin Stanton
14d. John Melia
15a. Ernest Rees
15b. Anthony Hughes
15c. Mary Lally
15d. Susan Douglas

16. Joseph Bowness
16a. Lilian Stanley
16b. Francis Connors
16c. Mary Woodhouse
16d. Marion Thomas
17. John Stanton
17a. Joseph Muscatelli
17b. Paulette Ward
17c. Andrew Doherty
17d. Francis Tasker
18a. Frances Griffin
18b. Thomas, Thomas jnr. & Mary Connor
18c. Bertha Glover
18d. John McGrail
19. Teresa Walsh
19a. Margaret Wrigley
19b. Mary Shiels
19c. Francis Carlyle
19d. Ellen Stack
20a. William Hughes
20b. William Christian
20c. John Boyle
20d. James Allen
21a. Mary Burford
21b. Martin Harkin
21c. Elizabeth Flaherty
21d. Edward Charters
22a. Christopher Kearney
22b. Catherine Moore
22c. Rosanna Smith
22d. Francis McCreith
23a. Walter Page
23b. Mary Shields
23c. Elizabeth O'Connell
23d. Catherine Conlon

CITIES BENEATH THE SEA
(J. Williams)

Paper cups and plastic bags, cast off clothing, turned to rags,
Toilet tissue by the ream, choke city streets and mountain stream.

Inside the mouths of rivers wide, rusting prams ride out the tide,
While strangely sluggish little fishes, snooze in long abandoned
dishes.

Splintered bottles and jagged tins, designed to quench an endless
thirst,
Lie in wait for exposed skin, to do their very worst.

Stream feeds the river that feeds the sea that feeds the clouds that
rain on me.

THE LEAVING OF LIVERPOOL
(Traditional)

Fare thee well to Princes landing stage, River Mersey, fare thee well,
I am bound for Californ-i-a- from a place I know true well.

So fare thee well, my own true love, when I return, united we will be,
It's not the leaving of Liverpool that grieves me,
But my darling, when I think of thee.

Fare thee well to Lower Frederick Street, Anson Terrace and old
Park Lane,
For I know it will be a long, long time, before I see you all again.

So fare thee well, my own true love, when I return, united we will be,
It's not the leaving of Liverpool that grieves me, but my darling
when I think of thee.

I hope you have enjoyed the book. Why not drop a line to the Scottie Press forum on www.scottiepress.org I am always interested in photographs of the areas covered. If you have any or any feedback on this book, I would be pleased to hear it.

Gerard Fagan.